This is
SOUTH AFRICA

W9-BZF-124

This is
SOUTH AFRICA

Peter Borchert

First published in the UK in hardcover in 1993 by
New Holland (Publishers) Ltd
86–88 Edgware Road W2 2EA London, United Kingdom
www.newhollandpublishers.com
First published in softcover in the UK in 2000

ISBN 978 1 85974 282 2
10 9 8

Text © Peter Borchert 1993, 1995, 2000
Map © Struik Publishers
Photographs © 1993, 1995, 2000 individual photographers and/or
their appointed agents listed on page 160. Front cover photograph
© Gerald Cubitt 2000; spine photograph © Peter Pickford, Images of
Africa 2000

All rights reserved. No part of this publication may be reproduced,
stored in a retrieval system or transmitted in any form or by any
means, electronic, mechanical, photocopying, recording or otherwise
without the prior written permission of the copyright owners.

Project co-ordinator: Marje Hemp
Copy editor (1993 edition): Peter Joyce
Copy editor (1995 edition): Brenda Brickman
Designer: Tamsyn Ivey
Cover designer: Tracey Mackenzie
Typesetting by Suzanne Fortescue, Struik DTP, Cape Town
Reproduction by Hirt & Carter (Cape) Pty Ltd
Printed and bound by Times Offset (M) Sdn Bhd, Malaysia

FRONT COVER: *The Hex River Valley between Worcester
and Touws River.*
SPINE PICTURE: *A male lion.*
FRONTISPIECE: *Sunset on a farm in the Kamberg district,
KwaZulu-Natal.*
OVERLEAF: *Trout fishing on Lake Navarone in the Drakensberg.*
OPPOSITE: *Table Mountain, one of the world's most familiar land-
marks, flanked by Devil's Peak (left) and Lion's Head (right).*

Over 40 000 unique African images available to purchase from our
image bank at www.imagesofafrica.co.za

SOUTH AFRICAN PROFILE

The association of a people with the land they live in is always difficult to understand. This is particularly so in countries where national, regional and local affairs, together with a number of strong cultural identities create an intricate web of allegiances and affiliations. At this point in its history, South Africa is even more complex than most as it enters the new century, albeit sometimes rather uncertainly, but with a sense of great hope, the likes of which the country and all its people have never before experienced. Re-admittance into the world community and the relative speed, peace and goodwill with which the country has created a new order have been heady experiences. A feeling of common purpose and national pride pervades, but it does not entirely mask the political and social divisions that lie beneath the thin veneer, and it would be a brave person, and probably a fairly stupid one, who would venture a tight definition and declare with confidence that 'This is South Africa'. Even an introductory essay such as this will, inevitably, run a gauntlet of criticism for bias, omission, over-simplification and prejudice.

For how can one tell the story of South Africa completely and to the satisfaction of all in the space of a few thousand words? Quite simply one cannot, and the text and captions for this book make no pretence at doing so. All that is offered is a series of glimpses, some more personal, others more broadly based, that will give the casual reader, particularly the newcomer or tourist, a few pointers to this endlessly fascinating and very lovely land of endless opportunity.

THE SHAPING OF THE LAND

South Africa is a very big country. Even its subdivisions into nine provinces are mostly sizeable, the exception being the densely populated economic and financial power-house of Gauteng, an almost continuous connurbation formed around the two major cities of Johannesburg and Pretoria.

The land, 1,2 million square kilometres in extent, sprawls from the Limpopo River in the north to the southern extremity of Cape Agulhas, where Africa peters out rather unimpressively in a jumble of low, windswept sand dunes and shallow reefs. South Africa's western shores are scoured by the cold waters of the Benguela Current driving up from the Antarctic, its eastern areas by the warm waters of the Agulhas Current sweeping down from the tropical Indian Ocean.

Even though one would expect a fair variety of landscapes in a country as large as South Africa, it is difficult to comprehend just how much physical diversity there is.

Reduced to simple terms, however, three major features determine the shape and the form of the land: a coastal plain that fringes the entire subcontinent; a vast inland plateau and, separating the two, an irregular chain of rugged mountains which, here and there, rather begrudgingly allows road and rail access between the coast and the interior.

In the east, and forming a great, virtually continuous escarpment running down from the Limpopo Province, across the northern limits of KwaZulu-Natal and then on into the Eastern Cape, is the mighty Drakensberg range. In KwaZulu-Natal, where the *Quathlamba* – the Zulu name for the range (the word means 'barrier of spears') – soar to heights of more than 3 000 metres, this alpine wilderness is at its most spectacular. In winter thick snow can blanket the peaks and often the lower slopes, briefly softening the rough face of Africa. But for most of the year the crags are bare and challenging, inviting legions of climbers and hikers.

In the Western Cape the mountain ranges are no less dramatic, but were borne of very different forces. More than 300 million years ago, when the continents were wrenching themselves free of the single land mass known as Pangaea, the heaving and buckling

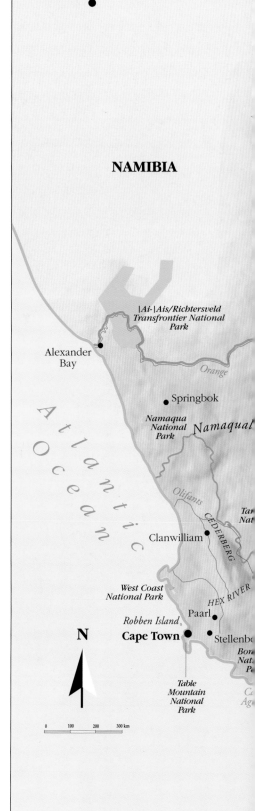

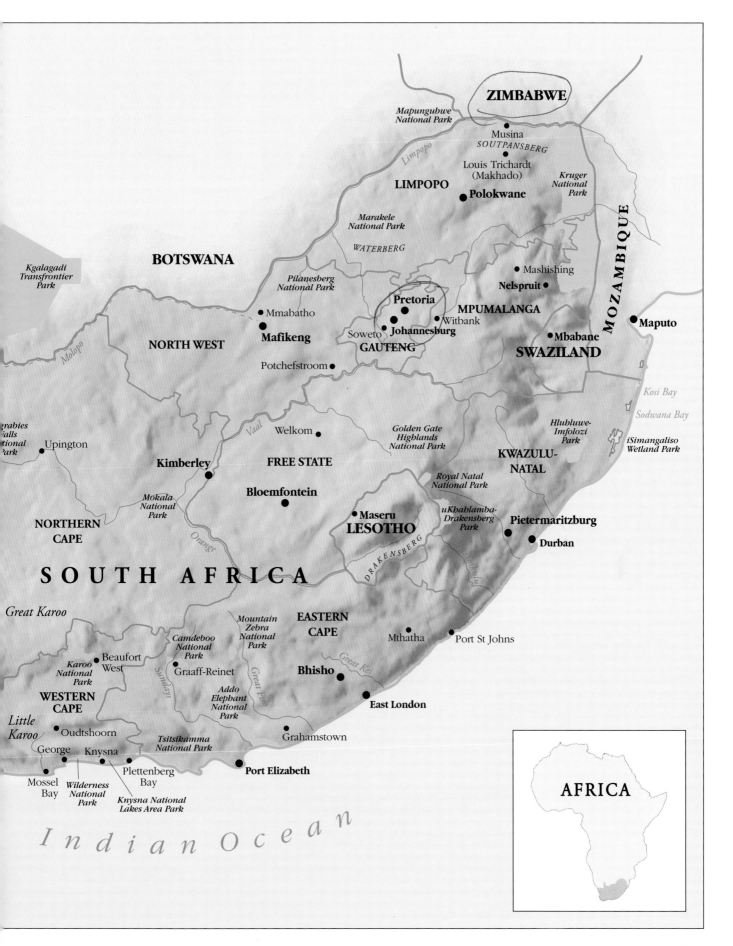

ZIMBABWE

Mapungubwe National Park

Musina

SOUTPANSBERG

Louis Trichardt (Makhado)

LIMPOPO

Kruger National Park

● Polokwane

Marakele National Park

WATERBERG

BOTSWANA

Kgalagadi Transfrontier Park

● Mashishing

Nelspruit ●

Pilanesberg National Park

MOZAMBIQUE

Pretoria

MPUMALANGA

● Mmabatho

Witbank

● Maputo

Soweto ● Johannesburg

● Mbabane

Mafikeng

GAUTENG

SWAZILAND

NORTH WEST

● Potchefstroom

Kosi Bay

Sodwana Bay

Molopo

Vaal

● Welkom

Golden Gate Highlands National Park

Hluhluwe-Imfolozi Park

...rabies ...lls ...tional ...rk

Upington ●

FREE STATE

KWAZULU-NATAL

iSimangaliso Wetland Park

Kimberley

Royal Natal National Park

Bloemfontein

Mokala National Park

● Maseru

uKhahlamba-Drakensberg Park

Pietermaritzburg

NORTHERN CAPE

LESOTHO

● Durban

Orange

DRAKENSBERG

SOUTH AFRICA

Great Karoo

Mountain Zebra National Park

EASTERN CAPE

Camdeboo National Park

Mthatha

Port St Johns

Karoo National Park

Beaufort West

Graaff-Reinet

Bhisho

Great Kei

WESTERN CAPE

Addo Elephant National Park

East London

Little Karoo

● Oudtshoorn

Tsitsikamma National Park

Grahamstown

George

Knysna

Mossel Bay

Wilderness National Park

Plettenberg Bay

● Port Elizabeth

Knysna National Lakes Area Park

I n d i a n   O c e a n

AFRICA

Merino sheep (left) graze in a Namaqualand pasture. Decorating a Little Karoo roadside is this colourful **trading store** (above). Cape Town's Bo-Kaap suburb is famed for its 18th-century **domestic architecture** (opposite).

earth threw up a range that would have dwarfed the Himalayas, and, although now a fraction of their former height, the legacy of the unimaginable forces that created them can be seen in the contorted rock strata of what are collectively known as the Cape Fold Mountains. On the seaward side of this escarpment the land is comparatively well watered: the Western Cape receives its share of rain mostly in winter, and the long months of summer are hot and dry; the subtropical east coast is subject to often monsoon-like summer downpours, creating sticky, steaming days with the evenings providing little relief. Along the southern coast, where forests – man-made and indigenous – clothe the landscape, the weather, mild for the most part, can be wet at any time of the year.

But rain is an irregular happening in Africa and the spectre of drought always looms. Although the coast can be hard hit, nowhere is the threat more real than on the vast interior plateau. Here, especially in the central and western parts, the rain falls sparingly even in the kinder seasons, dry periods sometimes lasting several years. During these times life is hard indeed. It is just such a waterless period that has followed many parts of Africa into the 1990s, causing crop failures, the death of livestock and game, and human misery on an unprecedented scale.

The South African hinterland – the plateau – is far from uniform in character and much of it is occupied by the Great Karoo. For some it is a bleak semi-desert to be traversed as quickly as possible, a penance for those headed for the pleasures of the seaside or returning home to the metropolises of the

north, but for others the endless scrubby plains, punctuated here and there with typically flat-crowned hills, or koppies, have a beauty all their own, where the sense of solitude can be an almost spiritual experience.

To the north of the Karoo the land continues to rise steadily in a series of low scarps across the Gariep (Orange) River, through the flat farms and goldfields of the central Free State and on over the Vaal River. Here the farms give way abruptly to mining, industry and the biggest coming together of people south of Cairo. This is Gauteng, a closely knotted string of towns, cities and suburbs with Johannesburg and Soweto at the centre, Pretoria in the north and Vereeniging in the south. Although a mere 1.4 per cent of South Africa's total area, nearly seven million people crowd into the conurbation. The only province with a greater population is KwaZulu-Natal which is some five-and-a-half times its area.

THE PEOPLING OF THE LAND

Exactly where, and precisely how long ago it was that hominid creatures first stood upright and began the long journey of descent to modern man, is the subject of endless debate by scientists, but there is sufficient evidence to suggest that Africa is the cradle of mankind. The archaeological surface of Africa, despite startling finds and deductions, has hardly been scratched and the progress of man remains largely hidden in the overburden of countless millennia.

Recent prehistory, though – the period of *Homo sapiens* – is a little clearer. There are

shellfish middens along the coast dating back 100 000 years, and sites such as Border Cave in northern KwaZulu-Natal, where arrowheads and ostrich eggshell beads have been found, showing that humans lived there more than 30 000 years ago. These early inhabitants of southern Africa were surely the ancestors of the Khoisan people who were here when the first Negroid Bantu-speakers arrived as part of an irregular, swirling migration spanning thousands of years, and which had its assumed origin in the region of the present-day state of Cameroon. Again the record is misted and incomplete, but we do know that by the 8th century copper mining by Bantu-speakers was well under way at Phalaborwa (on the border of the Kruger National Park) and that by the 11th century iron was being smelted in the heart of what is now Johannesburg.

Settlement of the eastern coastal regions of South Africa by Bantu-speaking people is thought to have begun as early as the 3rd century. These were the forebears of the Zulu- and Xhosa-speakers of today (who are closely related in their languages and culture) – the first indigenous Africans, other than the small, gracile Khoisan (a collective replacement for the terms Bushman and Hottentot, which have had pejorative connotations) encountered by the seafaring nations of western Europe in the early years of their long investigative association with the southern tip of Africa.

The full story of the early settlement of South Africa, notwithstanding the little we know for certain, would take volumes in the telling and even in the most succinct precis would need far more space than is available here. Suffice it to say that by the end of the 15th century, when the powers of western Europe began the prelude to their domination of South African affairs, a process they continued by way of their descendants to the recent present, the subcontinent was well settled by many people and cultures with ancient roots in the land.

THE PATH OF HISTORY

The course of recorded history at the southern tip of Africa begins with the navigation of its coastline by Portuguese seamen towards the end of the 15th century. It is possible, of course, that the Arabs, perhaps the Indians and the Chinese too, might have rounded the Cape before this. All had the technology to do so, but it seems unlikely that they did. And there may have been even earlier pathfinders. Herodotus, the Greek historian, records an expedition by Phoenicians and from this one can deduce that they did round the Cape, but there is no conclusive evidence.

Trade and commerce are more often than not the common denominator in man's exploration of his world. This certainly was the impetus for the Portuguese, and for the Dutch and British who were to follow them on what must have been a terrifying voyage. Even today, with state-of-the-art navigational equipment and regular weather reports, any sensible mariner has the deepest respect for the treacherous coastal waters of South Africa. The list of shipwrecks along the shoreline, and of those vessels lost farther out to sea, fill pages of the record books of Lloyds of London, and it continues to grow steadily.

The trading nations of Europe were well motivated to find alternatives to the established overland routes to the treasures of the East and of Africa.

But is was Portugal that provided the spark. First they took Ceuta from the Moors and then began the quest for West African gold. By the middle of the 15th century the Portuguese had reached the Senegal River, and in 1456 the Pope gave their sovereign full temporal and spiritual dominion 'from Cape Bojador and Nun, by way of Guinea and beyond, southwards to the Indies'. Of course, the indigenous people of these regions were not consulted in the matter, and thus began a long, uninterrupted period

of great European presumption over the affairs of Africa. It was in 1487, during the reign of João II, that Bartolomeu Dias set sail to find the way around the tip of Africa. He succeeded in doing so, but in a manner not of his choosing: he was storm-blown round the Cape without at first realizing it. He put ashore at Mossel Bay and then again farther along the coast to the east, but he failed to chart the final passage to India – an honour that belongs to Vasco da Gama, who as the century drew to a close successfully made the round trip to Goa and back.

Maritime expeditions along the route gradually became more regular, and so did the need to stop off at the Cape to replenish supplies of water and food. Thus it was only a matter of time before a permanent European settlement made its appearance at the Cape. It was not, however, the Portuguese who initiated the move. They had put roots down elsewhere – on the west and east coasts – and it was the Dutch, who had become successful competitors in the profitable markets of the Orient, who, in 1652, established the first permanent white outpost on the map of what is today South Africa. The commander of this small group was Jan van Riebeeck, whose statue stands at the foot of Adderley Street in Cape Town.

And so the beginnings of modern South Africa do not reside in the wealth of the country's gold, diamonds and other minerals, although this was to provide a later impetus to growth. They lie instead in the need to revictual the passing vessels of the powerful Dutch East India Company.

The grip of western agriculture on the unpromising soils of Africa was a tenuous one and there were many setbacks, but the settlement survived and steadily acquired an air of permanence. In due course some of the Company's employees were granted freehold over plots of land, and trade, despite opposition from the authorities, developed with the indigenous Khoisan people. Not surprisingly the Khoisan did not share the white man's notions of land tenure and stock ownership and, inevitably, there were disagreements. It was not long before the first official 'frontier' came into being – a thick hedge of wild almond trees, the remnants of which can be seen to this day along the watershed of Wynberg Hill. The Dutch were to remain in control of the Cape until

the end of the 18th century. Under their rule the initial settlement grew into a sizeable town with many fine buildings and wide dusty streets laid out around a series of noisome canals, or *grachten*. And of course there was the ever-present need for defence, at first in the shape of a rude mud and wood fort, later to be replaced by a strong stone castle surrounded by a moat. The design was that of the familiar five-starred bastions that were favoured at the time by the Dutch and other European powers.

Colonial farms spread outwards into the hinterland, many of their beautifully proportioned homesteads graced by elegant and often elaborate gables, built in what became known as the Cape Dutch style. Vines were planted; French Huguenots, refugees from religious persecution, arrived to make their home in the Franschhoek Valley; and the great interior began to be opened up to exploration, exploitation and to European influence. Slavery too, was a feature of the early colonial period: the local Khoisan were, in Dutch opinion, unsuitable as labour, and so slaves were imported, initially from other parts of Africa and then from the east. The descendants of these latter people are known as Cape Malays (most came not from Malaysia as their name would suggest, however, but from the Indonesian Archipelago) – a remarkably cohesive Muslim community that has given to Cape Town much of its colourful and cosmopolitan character.

*Queen Victoria gazes imperiously from the grounds of the **parliament buildings** (top) in Cape Town. South Africa's national flower is the **king protea** Protea cynaroides (above).*

The first Englishman to set foot on southern African soil was Sir Francis Drake: he dropped anchor and came ashore during his circumnavigation of the globe in 1580. But Britain was not to have any direct influence at the Cape, despite a futile attempt at its annexation in 1620, until the end of the 18th century, by which time the Dutch East India Company was in a hopeless financial state and the sun had well and truly set on the golden age of its mercantile dominance. France had declared war on Britain and the Netherlands and the Prince of Orange fled to London, where he was enveigled into surrendering the Cape on the understanding that it would be returned to him at the end of hostilities. It was not to be a long occupation, and in March of 1803 the territory was peaceably relinquished into the hands of the Dutch Batavian government.

The initial British stay may have been short but it was an important time in the life of the country. This was the age of local enlightenment and two of its most sparkling progeny, John Barrow, who arrived as secretary to the governor, Lord Macartney, and Lady Anne Barnard, wife of the colonial secretary and unofficial hostess for the governor, left a legacy of correspondence that gave fresh and often witty insight into the state and lively affairs of the Cape. The reluctant Macartney soon found himself embroiled in the vexing matters of far-flung, recalcitrant Dutch-speaking communities, notably in the far eastern reaches of the Cape Colony, where the pot was to simmer and regularly boil over for many decades.

The eastern frontier was a miserable and confused region: border disputes had led to tensions between white settlers and the Xhosa-speaking indigenous inhabitants; the Xhosa were at war both with themselves and with the Khoisan.

These troubles would haunt successive British administrations at the Cape when they returned. And return they did: in the early days of 1806, driven by fresh fears of French occupation (and probably also by concern over the prospect of American mercantile expansion) a formidable expeditionary force stood off Cape Town. Resistance by the Dutch garrison was brave but futile and after a short skirmish the British were back, this time to remain (though latterly with little authority) for the next century and a half – until 1961, when the then prime minister, Hendrik Verwoerd, led South Africa out of the British Commonwealth and down the path of 'grand apartheid' into a tragic time of isolation and oppression that was to last 30 long years.

When the British returned in 1806 the number of people under the direct or indirect control of the colonial authorities numbered some 50 to 60 000 – Europeans, Khoisan (Hottentots), slaves and growing numbers of people of mixed descent (the beginnings of the so-called 'coloured' community of South Africa). The numbers of Bantu-speaking people living beyond the proclaimed borders of the colony cannot be determined. But what is known is that they had highly sophisticated social structures and ancient value systems, including notions of land and cattle ownership that were poles apart from those of the expanding European culture, a contradistinction that could only lead to continuing strife along the shifting frontiers. The colonial government's plan to settle some 4 000 British immigrants along the Colony's eastern frontier, effected in 1820, only served to inflame the situation.

But the problem was not simply a matter of confrontation between the 'white' colony and 'black' Africa: the history of South Africa has never been that straightforward. Many of the Dutch settlers did not take kindly to British rule and communities located some distance from Cape Town were virtually laws unto themselves. Those in even more remote areas – the so-called trekboers – led semi-nomadic lives, constantly moving with their cattle to find suitable grazing. Their manner of living was not far removed from those of the black tribes with whom, down the years, they were so often in conflict and, although an unpalatable fact to hardened Afrikaner nationalists, some frontiersmen took common law black wives.

During the early decades of the second British occupation the movement for the emancipation of slaves gained ground, and in due course the parliament at Westminster decreed that slavery everywhere in the empire should be abolished. For many Dutch-speaking farmers at the Cape this was the last straw: the decision, coupled with a long list of other grievances against British rule, prompted an exodus from the colony of many families bonded together in a number of loose associations, each under a patriarchal leader. This migration in search of a promised land became known as the Great Trek, and the exploits and hardships of the trekkers as they drove their ox-drawn wagons across the plains and through the mountains to found their own republics – the Transvaal, the Orange Free State and, briefly, Natal – have been carved into the minds of South African school pupils, especially white Afrikaans-speakers, for the greater part of this century.

During this period, and before, the Xhosa-speaking peoples along the Cape frontier and farther eastward were divided, hampered from becoming a cohesive force against the colony, by their own internal struggles, a weakness that the British colonial government was all too quick to exploit to their own ends. Despite this, however, the British never managed entirely to suppress the clansmen across whichever river happened to be the border at the time, and indeed on a number of occasions the eastern parts of the colony came perilously close to being overrun.

In the end it was the Xhosa-speaking people who were to engineer their own tragic downfall. Believing the word of a young visionary, they destroyed their own cattle and other livestock, in the conviction that, by doing this, the ancestors would rise from the dead and drive the settlers and the British troops into the sea. This supreme act of faith led only to tragedy, as the prophecy was not fulfilled: instead, there was mass starvation and the destruction of the Xhosa-speaking nation as a political force, a powerlessness that lasted until well into the next century.

In what is today the province of KwaZulu-Natal, African history unfolded in a very different manner. Here, at the beginning of the 19th century, life in the hills and valleys at the foot of the Drakensberg was probably much the same as that among the Xhosa-speakers to the south west. But not for long: by the end of the second decade a young warrior, Shaka, the son of a minor chief, had begun to weld the clans into what was to become the Zulu nation, a military power unlike any the southern part of the continent had ever seen. Shaka was a ruthless genius who set about conquering, destroying and absorbing all those around him until he had established himself as undisputed king. Clans and others fleeing before his unstoppable armies made their way across the mountains and fell upon those living there to trigger what is called the *Difaqane*, or *Mfecane*, a chain of displacement and migration that reverberated across the highveld plains of southern Africa and up towards central Africa and beyond.

When the Dutch-speaking farmers, or Boers as they had come to be known, began their own migrations in the mid-1830s, the Zulu across the Drakensberg remained supreme under Shaka's successor, Dingane. On the grasslands of the high central plateau, a Zulu offshoot under the leadership of Mzilikazi, a brilliant military tactician who had fled the wrath of Shaka after falling from grace, had established an unrivalled power base. And it was against these two formidable fighting machines that the main thrusts of the Great Trek were directed. The battles were hard and bloody, but eventually gunpowder prevailed against spears, sheer numbers and raw courage. Mzilikazi moved northwards across the Limpopo to found the Matabele nation of present-day Zimbabwe, leaving the Boers to establish their republics. In Zululand, although beaten in battle, the Zulu people remained unbowed.

The Boers established a republic in the land of the Zulus, but it was shortlived: in 1842 British troops landed in Durban, where British settlers had gathered together a small trading and hunting community under the aegis of Shaka. The Boers responded by besieging the settlement, but with the arrival of British reinforcements from the eastern Cape they retired, most rejoining the central prong of the Great Trek. The British settled in to govern Natal, as the region had become known, and later to wage their own wars with the Zulus, who, in 1879, delivered some severe blows to the pride of the empire before submitting to superior weaponry.

And so, as the second half of the century progressed, the four provinces that until 1994 formed the basic structure of South Africa began to crystalize: the Cape and Natal under the British, and, to the north, the two Boer republics of the Transvaal and the Orange Free State.

The well-established antagonisms between the British and the Boers continued to fester, and the discovery of diamonds and gold in the northern parts of the country created the catalyst for open warfare between the Boers and the empire. The details of this bloody struggle have filled volumes – and filled minds with bitter memories that persist to the present. The outcome of the Anglo-Boer War, fought between 1899 and 1902, was eventual victory for Britain and an engineered Union of South Africa, formalized in May 1910 – an accommodation of the political aspirations of the white factions in South Africa with little or no reference to the rights, or wishes, of the black people who made up the greatest part of the country's population.

The politics that dominated the period from Union to the recent present have been those that entrenched increasing privilege for white South Africans and, for blacks, an unequal share in the prosperity that came with rapid industrialization. During this time Afrikaner nationalism grew to the point where, in the general election just after the Second World War, its leaders were able to wrest power from Jan Smuts, a man who, although an international statesman who had won the respect of the world (for a distinguished career that embraced contributions to the founding of the United Nations), was seen by many of his compatriots at home as a turncoat and traitor to the Afrikaner cause.

The new Nationalist government that came into power in 1948, and which remained in office until 1994, was responsible for

*The spontaneity of a child's smile (above) adds warmth to a **Johannesburg street scene.***

creating a South Africa unacceptable to the world and to the majority of its own citizens. The iron fist of apartheid closed ever tighter, removing black people from designated white areas, banning political movements that were seen as subversive, imprisoning their leaders and contriving for themselves an unassailable supremacy in the affairs of the land.

But, of course, the warped Utopia of white dominion over the economic wealth of the land, with black people neatly accommodated in their own homelands, was doomed from the start. International opinion, at first mildly censorious but increasingly vehement, rallied against a government flying defiantly in the face of a world moving rapidly away from imperialism and notions of racial supremacy.

Demonstrations of protest within the land were crushed with uncompromising harshness, but opposition could not be quelled indefinitely, and in 1976 the black township of Soweto erupted, sparking a countrywide chain reaction that forced the government to declare a state of emergency.

Concessions had to be made to restore order, and this was the turning point: the initial, modest compromises would eventually lead to an acknowledgement by the white government that a 'new South Africa' had to be negotiated with the resistance leaders who had been imprisoned, or driven into exile, or had gone underground.

*Johannesburg's streets are lively with colourful **fleamarkets** (above), a significant element of the vibrant 'informal economy'.*

POLITICAL TRANSITION

The pressures of isolation and international sanctions, and the realignment of the geo-political order after the collapse of the Soviet empire, prompted the National Party government to embark on fundamental and rapid reform. In a dramatic announcement in February 1990, State President F.W. de Klerk announced that the African National Congress (ANC), the Pan-Africanist Congress (PAC), the SA Communist Party (SACP) and other long-banned organizations would be free to conduct their business, and that political prisoners, including the ANC's Nelson Mandela – who had been incarcerated for the past 27 years – would be released. In so doing, De Klerk opened a way to reconciliation.

Mandela and the ANC responded in kind – not as revolutionaries whose time had come, but as visionaries determined on peaceful transition leading to a new South Africa.

The negotiations – conducted largely within the ambit of the Convention for a Democratic South Africa (Codesa) – proved long, hard, risky and plagued by setback after setback. Extremists at both ends of the political spectrum, but especially those on the right (among them a sinister, mysterious 'third force') did their best to sabotage the process. In 1992 alone an estimated 3 500 people died in political violence, including 30 ANC protesters on the borders of the 'independent' territory of Ciskei and 45 residents of the township of Boipatong, victims of a single senseless massacre. In April of the following year Chris Hani, the charismatic general secretary of the SACP and hero to the youth, fell to an assassin's bullet. Less dramatic but even more threatening was the absence from an otherwise all-inclusive Codesa of both the radical PAC and Chief Mangosuthu Buthelezi's Zulu-based Inkatha Freedom Party (IFP), whose agenda encompassed a healthy degree of independence for the Zulu homeland.

The chief protagonists, however, held firm. The major obstacle to agreement was the degree to which power would be shared in a future dispensation; the ANC insisted on simple 'winner-takes-all' majority rule along British constitutional lines, the Nationalists held out for a formula that blocked 'domination of one group by another', a euphemism for entrenched white minority rights. Both, however, remained flexible in their demands.

At the end of 1993 Parliament, an institution that still excluded black representatives, was effectively replaced by a Transitional Executive Council, which prepared the way for South Africa's first fully democratic national elections. Nelson Mandela and F.W. de Klerk, who had proved themselves to be not mere power-hungry politicians but statesmen of the highest order, shared the 1993 Nobel Peace prize, joining Archbishop Desmond Tutu in the elite band of South African laureates.

A few months later the country went to the polls in what proved to be, astonishingly, a tranquil, even cheerful electoral process to choose its new leaders. The ANC won just under two thirds of the votes, and on a sunny May day in 1995 Nelson Mandela mounted the podium at Pretoria's Union Buildings to be sworn in as South Africa's new State President, leader of a government of national unity and of a people filled with hope for the future.

If there is one word that encapsulates Mandela's presidency it is 'reconciliation' within what came to be known as the Rainbow Nation. A man of genuine humility, able to blend vision with a practical approach to the grim realities on the ground – deprivation, poverty, racial animosity, the bitter residues of decades of apartheid – he spearheaded the drive to bring people together. Perhaps the most crucial of his government's concessions to that reality was the decision to reject the socialist dictates of the Freedom Charter in favour of free-market principles. South Africa, in short, had chosen to join the modern world, with all its perils, challenges and rewards. And it did so with clean hands: a nomadic Truth and Reconciliation Commission assumed the role of a collective conscience, laid bare many of the sins of the past and has since served as a model for other communities around the world in search of a healing agent.

In a move rare among the leaders of Africa, Nelson Mandela voluntarily relinquished office at the end of the millennium. His protégé and successor, Thabo Mbeki, was well fitted for leadership: a gifted intellectual and competent technocrat, his managerial style and quiet diplomacy perfectly suited the needs of a country which, after the emotionally charged 'Mandela miracle' years, needed to get down the nuts and bolts of good governance. Mbeki's principal preoccupation has been what he calls the African Renaissance, a dream of continental rebirth through the agency of massive, globally sponsored investment.

WHERE THE PEOPLE LIVE

The common experience in developing countries world-wide is explosive population growth coupled with a seemingly uncontrollable rate of urbanization. Things are no different in South Africa: in recent years people have flooded to the cities, the rate accelerated by the relaxation of previous restrictions on where black people could live, and by rural hardship brought about by protracted drought, and almost non-existent employment opportunities. The country's population is currently about 40 million, and while estimates of average growth are unreliable, some analysts forecast that the figure will double within the next 30 years and that most of these some 80 million people will be urbanized. Already Durban is reputed to be among the fastest growing cities in the world, with Cape Town not far behind.

The consequences of such growth will be critical, not least on the environment. Already urban resources cannot cope, and in rural areas the rate of deforestation is way beyond the capacity of the environment to recover: if current rates continue the former so-called tribal homelands will be completely denuded of trees by the year 2020.

In the context of these dynamics any attempt to describe neatly how and where South Africans live is impossible, but some broad brush strokes will perhaps be useful.

Of the cities of the Western and Eastern Cape, Cape Town is the largest (it is also, at present, the legislative capital of the country), followed by Port Elizabeth and East London.

In KwaZulu-Natal the economic focus is the port of Durban, followed by the smaller, provincial capital of Pietermaritzburg 90 kilometres inland. Together, these two centres form an almost continuous corridor of industry and urban development beyond which – apart from the port of Richards Bay, nearby Empangeni and the northern coal mines and power generating plants – KwaZulu-Natal is almost entirely rural. Although agriculture is diverse the most prolific farming activity is sugar.

Sugar farming in KwaZulu-Natal had begun in the mid-19th century and, because the Zulu tribesmen were reluctant to work in the cane fields, labour was indentured from India. At the end of their periods of contract Indian families were given the opportunity to return home, but many decided to stay to form the basis of what is today a strong Indian presence in all sectors of KwaZulu-Natal society.

More than anything, though, KwaZulu-Natal is the home of the Zulu people. The Zulu royal family is still very much a force in the traditional and cultural lives of Zulu people, but real political power rests with Mangosuthu Buthelezi and his Inkatha Freedom Party.

The Free State lies within the converging arms of the Gariep (Orange) River in the south and the Vaal River to the north, and the only urban settlement of real size is its capital, Bloemfontein, also the seat of the country's highest judicial authority. Formerly a stronghold of white conservatives, political power is now – as it is everywhere in the country with the exception of KwaZulu-Natal – firmly in the hands of the ANC. White, largely Afrikaans-speaking farmers still hold considerable economic power in the province where much of the land is given over to maize farming. The Free State is also gold-mining country, the centre of its goldfields the town of Welkom.

North of the Free State lie the four provinces that now comprise what was the Transvaal – Limpopo Province, Gauteng, Mpumalanga and North-West. The smallest of the four, but the undisputed hub of industrial and financial activity, not only for the area but

the country as a whole, is Gauteng, described earlier in this introduction. But the tentacles of industry reach out far beyond the cities, for nowhere in these northern regions of South Africa is one far removed from mining, power generation and steelmaking. To the west of Gauteng lie the goldfields, among which are the deepest mines in the world; to the east, strung out across the plains, are the cooling towers of giant thermal power stations fed by huge, opencast coal mines. The provinces are also host to many other mining operations, including platinum and iron ore. But they are also farm and ranch land and big game country. The latter is a specially prominent feature of the far east, where the high escarpment drops away to the Lowveld and the domain of the world famous Kruger National Park.

Politically the provinces north of the Vaal embrace the full spectrum of affiliations, from ultra right-wing white rural communities to the foment of uncompromising black nationalism in the townships of the Witwatersrand, from the moderate Afrikaner establishment in Pretoria, the administrative seat of the country, to the white liberalism of Johannesburg's wealthy northern suburbs. Although the boundaries of these societies have begun to blur, it will take generations, if at all, for them to disappear.

THE ROAD AHEAD

South Africa's first government since the April 1994 elections has had to grapple with a nightmarish number of crucial social and economic issues. And the struggle is likely to continue for many years if South Africa is to find its way back on the road towards prosperity. Housing, education and employment problems have to be addressed. The basic infrastructure is in place – airports, harbours, rail and road systems, power, telecommunications, water storage schemes and raw materials – but huge funds are required, not only for the grand schemes but also to foster an entrepreneurial spirit among ordinary people. These funds could be forthcoming, not only from within the country but by way of foreign investment: the potential for industrial and commercial growth is enormous. But money will not flow unless the country can prove to potential investors and benefactors that a free and open economy, as well as a social stability and general political accord that is binding on all South Africans, can be acheived and maintained.

*Mining and mineral processing are among South Africa's key economic sectors. Here, **molten metal** (top) is poured at a Highveld steelworks; **coalminers** (above) emerge from a shift underground.*

South Africa is blessed with more than its share of the world's mineral wealth, but its priceless flora and fauna, coupled with some of the most majestic scenery in the world, are the real jewels in its crown. Although the country represents a mere 0,8 per cent of the world's landmass, it is home to more than 8 per cent of all known plantlife, 8 per cent of all birdlife, and nearly 6 per cent of the world's mammals ... the list goes on. Moreover a high proportion of these species occur nowhere else. For example, the plants of the Western Cape are so different from those in other parts of the world that this tiny piece of land has been defined as one of the six floral kingdoms of the world, ranked equally with the Boreal Kingdom, more than 1 000 times bigger, that includes all of Europe, North America and northern Asia. This indescribable richness, if properly preserved, could be the platform for a tourist industry that would far outstrip industry and mining in the country as the premier earner of foreign capital.

Turning a natural area into a playground for the privileged few is no longer an option. For conservation and for the tourist industry built around it to succeed, the people themselves have to benefit directly, and to have a voice in the development of such resources.

*The afterglow of sunset settles over **Hillbrow** (right), Johannesburg's densely populated flatland. To the west of this inner suburb is the trendy **Market Theatre** (top), a sort of South African Covent Garden where once derelict market buildings have been given a new and purposeful lease on life. The area around the complex is a hive of activity – especially at the weekend fleamarket, when the air is alive with the sounds of busking musicians.*

Glittering like a diamond set in the city of gold is **11 Diagonal Street** (left), a sleek, modern building reflecting the old and the new. The street is at the heart of Johannesburg's financial district, the imposing buildings of giant corporations standing in stark contrast to a huddle of old single- and double-storey shops where anything – from hi-fi's, top hats and jewellery to muti from a traditional herbalist – can be bought. The area, too, is one of the many terminuses for the never-ending rows of **minibus taxis** (top left) that ferry people back and forth between the city and the fringing townships.

Southgate (top right), one of Johannesburg's legion of shopping complexes, serves the city's southern suburbs, most of which are downmarket, a few of them smart – though none compares with the quiet opulence of **Houghton** (above), where gracious, sprawling homes, including Nelson Mandela's, are set against lawns that, from the air, have the appearance of tree-lined fairways.

*Johannesburg's Crown Mines, which yielded well over a million kilograms of gold during its long and honourable life, was until recently one of the numerous derelict workings that fringe the city's southern areas, their rusting headgears silent monuments to the pioneering past. An imaginative reconstruction scheme, however, has transformed the site into the popular **Gold Reef City** theme park (above), an evocative if romanticized re-creation of the early days in the Transvaal goldfields.*

*A Victorian funfair, museums, speciality shops and restaurants are just a few of the attractions on offer at Gold Reef City. Here one can also explore the early underground workings, see **gold being poured** (top left) and watch miners performing their recreational **traditional dances** (right).*

No-one can pretend that Johannesburg is a beautiful city, but what it lacks in visual quality it more than makes up for in verve and character: the arts flourish, the social scene is lively, and the

commercial sector is dynamic and imaginative, its pride the vast, modern shopping centres that bring glittering sophistication to the surrounding suburbs. Ranking first among this is the huge Sandton City complex which embraces the opulent Sandton Sun and Sandton Towers hotels.

Not to be outdone, however, is this new development at **Bruma Lake** (top right), a complex of pubs, restaurants and specialty shops set beside a splendid artificial water feature.

*P*retoria, administrative capital of South Africa, is famed for its broad, **jacaranda-lined avenues** (top). In spring and early summer the jacaranda trees burst into bloom, making glorious lilac tunnels of the city's thoroughfares. Ironically the jacaranda is not a South African species: the first few specimens were imported from Rio de Janeiro in 1888.

Museums, monuments to both the republican and colonial past, and imposing public buildings abound in Pretoria, as do beautifully laid out parks and

gardens. Pretoria's handsome **Melrose House** (left), where, in 1902, Boer and British Imperial leaders gathered to sign the Treaty of Vereeniging, bringing to an end the bitterly fought and hugely destructive South African War. Eight years later, in May 1910, they came together again to create the Union of South Africa.

Among Pretoria's most striking public landmarks are the splendidly proportioned **Union Buildings** (above), designed by celebrated British architect

Sir Herbert Baker, completed in 1913 and destined to serve as the model for the much larger but no more graceful seat of Imperial government in New Delhi. The neo-classical, crescent-shaped sandstone edifice overlooks Pretoria from the heights of Meintjes Kop; the statue is that of General Louis Botha, the Union's first prime minister.

The Union Buildings formed the imposing backdrop to President Nelson Mandela's inauguration on May 10, 1995, an event televised worldwide.

A **Ndebele matron** *in traditional dress stands at the entrance to her rural home near Pretoria. The highly elaborate garb and the* **geometric murals** *(left and top) are distinctive of Ndebele culture. The vividly coloured blanket, seemingly cumbersome hoops and intricately beaded apron are of consider-able weight, but the whole ensemble is worn without obvious discomfort. Ndebele women traditionally shave their heads, and the brass rings adorning neck, arms and legs are seldom, if ever, removed.*

The decorative murals are almost exclusively the preserve of Ndebele womenfolk, who practise their painting skills from puberty onwards. The striking colours are more a reflection of the availability of cheap, factory produced paints than of tradition, which encompassed the use of natural materials to produce softer, more earthy tones.

To the west of Pretoria lie the Magaliesberg, a lovely range of hills that cradle **Hartbeespoort Dam** *(above), a popular weekend retreat.*

*For over a decade now, the huge Sun City resort complex, which includes the **Cascades Hotel** (top right), has been one of southern Africa's top tourist drawcards, a place to gamble, a place to take in stage extravaganzas and a place to play — especially golf on the superb Gary Player designed course, venue each December for the Million Dollar Challenge. The glittering complex, with its unlikely setting in the middle of the North-West Province's scrubby countryside, is the brainchild of South*

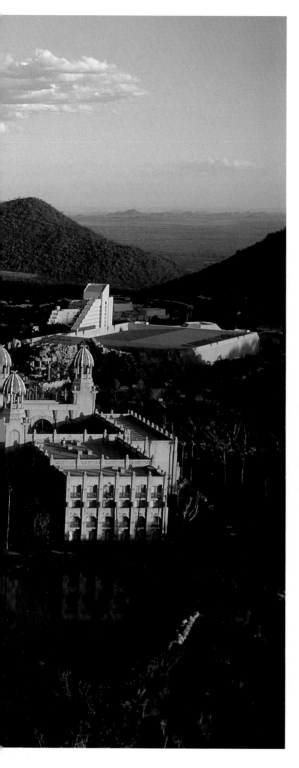

Africa's hotel genius, Sol Kerzner, who, in an expression of unbridled optimism for the tourism potential of the country, opened the **Lost City** (above, centre and left) in a blaze of international press and television publicity. The Lost City, an ultra-luxurious African fantasy, cost more than R800 million. In complete contrast to the glitz of the Sun City complex, is the nearby Pilanesberg National Park, a 50 000-hectare game sanctuary which lies in an ancient volcanic crater.

The Mpumalanga escarpment, where the high inland plateau drops – in places dramatically – to the steamy subtropical Lowveld, is among the most scenically beautiful regions of the country. One of the many passes leading down into the bushveld plain winds through the **Magoebaskloof** (above), just to the west of the immensely fertile Letaba region. Although picturesque, the **wattle and pine** plantations (right) that green so many of the slopes are a poor environmental substitute for the indigenous forests that are under threat. The **green pigeon**, Treron calva, (top right) is a resident of the escarpment woodland, where it is often seen in small groups clambering, parrot-like, among the foliage in search of fruit.

Waterfalls abound along the escarpment. Many, such as the beautiful cascade of **Debengeni** (top left), have deep dark pools at their feet, said by locals to be the resting places of ancestral spirits, legends which are not difficult to believe.

*O*ne of the least spoilt and scenically most splendid parts of the north-eastern escarpment region is the **Wolkberg** (above), a rugged wilderness area that harbours remnants of once extensive natural forests. Here, and all along the escarpment, fast-flowing streams tumble over their rocky floors as they race downhill, often leaping over the edges of cliffs in spectacular high cascades and elsewhere forming tranquil pools to invite the **angler** (top).

The watercourses of Mpumalanga are renowned
for their fierce-fighting trout, and fly-fishing has
become a favoured pastime among Johannesburg's
rich and leisured, many of whom are regular visitors to the exclusive fishing lodges and country
hotels of the region.

Another burgeoning pastime in this scenic area
is **hiking** (above). Crisscrossing the escarpment are
trails ranging from gentle rambles to more arduous
routes that challenge even the hardiest adventurers.

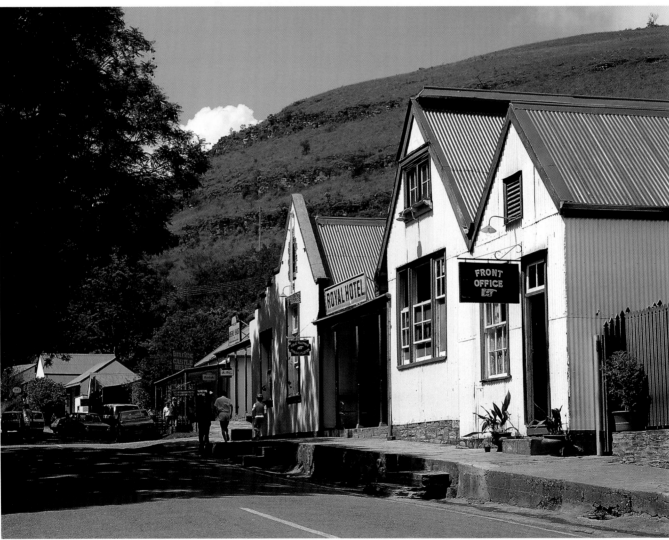

In 1873 gold was discovered in the highlands of Mpumalanga, and with the news came the inevitable motley crew of adventurers that have enlivened goldrush territories through the centuries. They arrived from all corners of the world to search the hills, many of them only to succumb to bad luck, despair and booze. But one of the upland streams yielded particularly worthwhile deposits of the yellow metal, and the tents and rude shacks of the initial workings soon gave way to a permanent settlement, which the diggers named **Pilgrim's Rest** (above). Today the village, a quaint collection of wood-and-iron buildings, still flourishes, but as a 'living museum' for the busloads of tourists who come to explore the past and to browse through the bric-a-brac and mining memorabilia offered for sale at the **general dealer's store** (top).

Not far from Pilgrim's Rest, near the village of Graskop, are the majestic **Lisbon Falls** (right), a favourite resting place and picnic site for tourists.

The **Blyde River Canyon** (left), the only true canyon in South Africa, is one of the country's grandest natural features: in places it drops almost sheer for 800 metres from the rim of red sandstone cliffs to the water below.

Over millions of years the relentless action of wind and water have weathered the gorge's edge to create a fantasy world of peaks and buttresses, many of which, like the **Three Rondavels** (above), bear highly descriptive names.

The Motlatse River continues its flow northwards until it meets the Olifants, one of the major perenial watercourses that are the lifeblood of the Kruger National Park. Closer towards the Motlatse's source is another confluence – with the Sefogane – and here nature has carved a second, though lesser, wonder: a hydraulic hammer of boulders and moving water has eroded the sandstone into a confusion of deep crevices known as **Bourke's Luck Potholes** (top), named after Tom Bourke, an early prospector.

The Kruger National Park, without doubt the country's best known and most popular wildlife refuge, sprawls across the Mpumalanga Lowveld, covering an area that is larger than many of the world's countries. More than 600 000 visitors a year come from all around the globe to enjoy what must be one of the greatest of outdoor experiences. The tourist figures would seem to suggest over-crowding and close contact with fellow travellers at every turn, but once out of the main camps the

bush simply swallows them up, and one can travel long distances without sight of another vehicle or human being. The sense of solitude one feels in the bush is especially acute at the **Olifants Camp** (left), in the central region of the Park. Here, seen from the hilltop lookout, a vast landscape of trees and scrub stretches to the far horizons.

The monotony of the northern Kruger's endless mopane woodlands is occasionally broken by a majestic **baobab**, Adansonia digitata (above).

Baobabs are true symbols of Africa, growing to massive sizes and great age – specimens with trunks 30 metres in diametre and thought to be as old as 4 000 years are known.

For the wealthier visitor to the Lowveld, a number of privately run lodges along the Kruger's western boundary, such as **Sabi Sabi** (top left), offer an enticing combination of personalized game-viewing from open vehicles, luxury accommodation and superb cuisine – the ultimate African experience.

*T*he elevated Tree Camp at the **Londolozi lodge** *(above) provides a secure and very comfortable vantage from which to absorb the sights and sounds of the bush.*

*A glimpse of a **leopard**, Panthera pardus, (left) may perhaps be the reward of patience – Londolozi is famed for its studies of this secretive cat, which are compellingly captured on film and in a superb book – but even if the larger wild animals are not forthcoming the surrounding bushveld provides* *an endless source of wonder. For example, the delicate structure and colours of the flowers of the **sickle bush**, Dichrostachys cinerea, (top left) or a **tree squirrel**, Paraxerus cepapi, (top right) scampering down a tree, or an **emperor moth**, Argema sp., (above) its characteristically furry, fragile green wings all but indistinguishable from its leafy habitat, are precious gems too easily missed in the often frenetic quest for the 'big five' – lion, leopard, elephant, rhino and buffalo.*

Mala Mala is one of the internationally renowned upmarket private reserves that lie adjacent to the Kruger National Park, and a casual perusal of its visitor's book would reveal a litany of the world's rich and famous. A few days and nights at Mala Mala are sure to bring the excitement of seeing, close up, all the large inhabitants of the reserve, whether on an easy, ranger-guided walk down to the river to watch **hippo**, Hippopotamus amphibius *(left)*, or on a game drive through the almost park-like bushveld where **buffalo**, Syncerus caffer, *(left centre)* and **waterbuck**, Kobus ellipsiprymnus, *(above)* with their shaggy grey coats and tell-tale white 'lavatory seat' markings around their rumps, are to be seen.

Of the five species of bee-eaters found in the Lowveld, two are common residents: the little bee-eater, and the **whitefronted bee-eater**, Merops bullockoides, *(left top)*. All members of this family are brightly coloured and can be easily seen.

A group of sub-adult **lions** *(left), their youth revealed by spots – which usually disappear by maturity – still faintly visible on their flanks. The lion,* Panthera leo, *is the largest and most powerful of the African cats: full grown males can attain more than three metres in length and weigh more than 200 kilograms.*

*The magnificent **martial eagle***, Polemaetus bellicosus, *(above) photographed here with its prey, is just one of the Lowveld's many raptors.*

*T*he *timeless sequence: another bushveld day
ends with the sinking sun sending soft light
through a haze of fine dust (right).*

*Although these **buffalo** (top left) seem peaceable
enough, the species is well known for its unpredict-
ability and sometimes for its aggression, and
campfire gatherings abound with tales, real and
imaginary, of close encounters with these animals.
The **wild dog**, Lycaon pictus, (top right) is also a
victim of bad publicity, and is regarded by many*

*as a vicious killer. A closer understanding of the
species, however, shows that a pack will hunt only
for its immediate needs and that the animals lead
a highly complex and structured community life.
For example, individuals returning from a successful kill will regurgitate meat for their young as well
as for those who remained behind, either to guard
the home den or because they were injured.*

*A herd of **elephants**, Loxodonta africana, (above)
moves in an unhurried procession through the veld.*

*T*hree **cheetahs** *(above) lap in unison at a bush-veld stream. The cheetah,* Acinonyx jubatus, *is sometimes confused with the* **leopard** *(top right), but the dog-like face and muzzle and the heavy tear marks down the former's cheeks, which give the cat its somewhat mournful countenance, are distinctive identifying features.*

Unlike the other big cats which tend to be noctur-nal and to rely on stealth, a short charge and sheer brute strength to overcome their prey, the cheetah,

because of its light frame, cannot bring down large animals. Its breathtaking acceleration, however – in full cry speeds of more than 70 kilometres an hour are attained – and superb balance are often more than a match for the swift, darting runs of the smaller antelope that are its main prey.

A mixed herd of **Burchell's zebra,** Equus burchellii, and **blue wildebeest**, Connochaetes taurinus, (above) at a waterhole; some of the animals drink while others keep a wary eye out for predators.

*The **giraffe**, Giraffa camelopardalis, (above) may seem ungainly, but anyone who has witnessed the effortless ease with which the animal glides over the ground at full gallop will immediately appreciate the appropriateness of its common name, which derives from the Arabic word* xirapha, *meaning 'the one who walks swiftly'. This long-necked browser is the tallest of all animals, an evolutionary development which gives them sole feeding rights over the high foliage of the bushveld trees. Also a browser,*

but feeding on a range of vegetation much closer
to the ground, is the lovely **nyala**, Tragelaphus
angasii, *(above)*. The difference between the sexes
of this handsome antelope is very obvious: the larger
males have long, lyre-shaped horns and dark shaggy
coats while the much smaller females are hornless
and are considerably lighter in colour.

Also part of the bushveld tapestry are the exquisite
impala lily, Adenium obesum, *(top right)* and the
ubiquitous **chacma baboon**, Papio ursinus *(top left)*.

The landlocked province of the Free State, which lies on the high central tableland in the very heart of South Africa, is for the most part flat and featureless, its great plains devoid of trees. But the soils are rich, and in years of good summer rains the endless rows of maize grow tall and golden, and vast fields of sleepily nodding **sunflowers** (top left) stretch to the far horizons. But when the rains fail and drought descends on the land, the countryside becomes a dustbowl, its topsoils borne

*away on the hot, dry winds. In such times and in the raw cold of winter the **windmills** (left) work ceaselessly to bring life-sustaining water from deep subterranean reservoirs.*

*Towards the east, where the republic meets the mountain kingdom of Lesotho, the landscape is a lot more interesting, the skyline broken by isolated, flat-topped **sandstone buttes** (above) and the country-side brightened by an occasional **scatter of huts** (top right) decorated according to local custom.*

*Winter landscape: **merino sheep** (top) stand silhouetted against the early morning mist. Although these tall, exotic **poplars** (above) may offend the environmental purist, their autumn foliage paints an idyllic pastoral scene. The poplars are prominent in the far north-eastern corner of the Free State, and are even found among the otherwise indigenous flora of the Golden Gate Highlands National Park, where they blend well with the burnt hues of the **sandstone cliffs** (right).*

The mighty Drakensberg range is a continuation of the great rocky escarpment that begins in the Limpopo Province and extends around the entire rim of the country. Nowhere is this mountainous ridge more dramatic than in northern KwaZulu-Natal, where an alpine world of high crags and breathtaking precipices falls for a full 2 000 metres down to the green and pleasant coastal plain.

Looking out across the spines of the 'dragon mountain' or 'barrier of spears', one can see, rising above the cloud, the **Eastern Buttress** and its attendant **Devil's Tooth** (left), while two hikers take a hard-earned rest (above) on **Injasuti Peak**.

This magnificent **black eagle**, Aquila verreauxii, (top left) is poised to take its favoured prey, the rock hyrax, or 'dassie', Procavia capensis.

The Bushmen, or San, are long gone from the Drakensberg, but their spirit remains in their marvellously evocative **rock art** (top right), of which thousands of examples are to be found.

The **Amphitheatre** (previous page), rising
3 000 metres and more above sea level, is one
of the Drakensberg's best known features and is a
magnet for the more intrepid mountaineer. It also
provides the imposing backdrop to the Royal Natal
National Park, an 8 000-hectare sanctuary famed
for its spectacular scenery, its plant life and its
birds of prey. The park offers pleasant accommodation in its **Tendele Camp** (right) from where an
excursion up Mont-aux-Sources and the spectacular

Tugela Falls is but one of many options for the energetic walker. The flora and fauna of the high 'Berg and its foothills are extraordinarily rich, and much of the region is accessible through thoughtfully planned hiking ways. Paths and tracks are carefully contoured to keep soil erosion to a minimum; **suspension bridges** (top) have been built over the many streams and ravines. Guided **horse trails** in the Giant's Castle area (left) are also very popular.

*T*he formidable crags and pinnacles of the
Devil's Knuckles *(right), bathed in the soft,
clear light of a Drakensberg winter's morning.
The Drakensberg of KwaZulu-Natal and the sandstone cliffs of the eastern Free State are among the
few remaining refuges in the world for the* **lammer-
geier***, Gypaetus barbatus, (top) and a sighting of
it could well be the reward of taking to one of the
many* **hiking trails** *in the 'Berg (above) or visiting
the vulture 'restaurant' at Giant's Castle.*

*The view across the **Drakensberg**, looking
north from Cathedral Peak (left). Below the
peak lies a resort hotel – one of many established
among the foothills – which provides a comfortable
base for exploring the surrounding countryside or
just relaxing in the rarefied mountain air. Or you
can take your enjoyment the hard way, like these
entrepid **hikers** (above) huddled against the bone-
chilling cold that can descend with the night,
even in the height of summer.*

*The gently rolling hills of the KwaZulu-Natal midlands, and their beauty and tranquillity, belie their turbulent past. For much of the 19th century this region served as the great battleground of South Africa: it was here, in the years after 1818, that Shaka's impis emerged in all their disciplined magnificence to subdue, and to absorb, the neighbouring Nguni peoples and thus to lay the foundations of the mighty Zulu empire. Later the Zulu fought, and in due course succumbed to, two well-armed invaders: the Voortrekkers from the Cape (in 1838) and a British army bent on territorial conquest (in 1879). Today the midlands are still subject to sporadic strife as ancient feuds and latter-day political rivalries are played out. To the passing traveller, however, these realities are largely hidden from view, belonging to a world far apart from the yachts bobbing benignly on **Midmar Dam** (above) and the timeless serenity of the **Howick Falls** (right), over which the waters of the Mgeni River tumble.*

Much of KwaZulu-Natal's colonial past can be seen in the provincial capital of Pietermaritzburg – although, ironically, the elegant little city was named after two Boer heroes of the Great Trek, Piet Retief and Gert Maritz.

In 1843 Natal was annexed by the British, but it was to be fully half a century before the colony was granted responsible government, at which time a gracious **House of Assembly** (above) made its appearance. After Union in 1910 the assembly became the seat of the Provincial Council. With the fine old building at her rear, Queen Victoria continues to cast her proprietary gaze over a region which, not always jokingly, is often referred to by locals and outsiders alike as 'the last outpost of the British Empire'.

The **City Hall** (left), which was also built towards the end of the 19th century, boasts a handsome clock tower and is reputedly the largest all-brick building in the southern hemisphere.

Although the old ways of the Zulu people are fast disappearing under the pressures of urbanization and the onslaught of Western culture, in the remote hills and valleys of Zululand tradition is still strong on ceremonial occasions. Here a **Zulu maiden** (top), festooned with elaborate beadwork, has her hair tightly plaited with strips of bright red cloth, while two young men (above) display their prowess at **stick fighting**. Other legacies of the past are to be found in the rituals attendant on coming of age and of marriage, in the body of animistic belief, and in the splendid choral music for which the Zulu-speaking people are renowned.

The characteristic 'beehive' huts of a traditional Zulu homestead deep in the **Valley of a Thousand Hills** (right). It was near here, at the confluence of the Mhlatuze and Mvazana rivers, that, in 1819, the young Shaka defeated the Ndwandwe, a decisive milestone in his rise to power and undisputed dominion over much of present-day KwaZulu-Natal.

*Diviners – intermediaries between the ancestral spirits and their living descendants – continue to play an important role in the everyday lives of many ordinary Zulu people, and the advice of the sangoma is frequently sought on a wide range of medical and social issues. This **young diviner** (left), is still an apprentice, her status indicated by her white-painted face.*

Shakaland, near the town of Eshowe, is a Zulu cultural village where tourists can observe and –

*to a degree – experience traditional lifestyles. Accommodation is provided in comfortably fitted out beehive huts, while a **pub and a restaurant** (top) cater to western tastes. Among the many crafts displayed here are beadworking, pottery and **spear making** (above), in which metal blades are worked over an open fire and then honed to a keen edge on a suitable stone. The few traditional craftsmen and women who continue to ply their trade do so principally for the tourist industry.*

*E*vening falls at **Ntshondwe Lodge** (above) in the Itala Game Reserve. Itala, which lies northeast of Vryheid in northern KwaZulu-Natal, is a triumph for the efforts of the KwaZulu-Natal Nature Conservation Service: this hilly reserve was proclaimed in 1972 and since then many large mammals long extinct in the area have been reintroduced, including **Burchell's zebra**, Equus burchellii, (top left) and the **giraffe**, Giraffa camelopardalis, (top right). Both animals also occur in the Mkuzi

Game Reserve, nearer the coast to the east, which is regarded by many as the jewel in the crown of KwaZulu-Natal's conservation areas. For its size Mkuzi certainly offers splendid game-viewing, and visitors could well be rewarded with sightings of both black and white rhino. The savanna woodland extending across the reserve is dotted with majestic trees, among the more prominent being the **umbrella thorn**, Acacia tortilis, (above) which, with the possible exception of the baobab, is the tree of Africa.

*M*kuzi has much to offer the game-viewer, but it is for the avid bird-watcher that the reserve has a special magic. More than 400 species are known to occur here; Nsumu and **Nhlonhlela** (above) pans are famous for such waterbirds as the unmistakably marked **pygmy goose**, Nettapus auritus, (right, centre). Amphibian life is also prolific and includes the delicate **tinker reed frog**, Hyperolius tuberilinguis, (top right). The sun sets over a pan in Mkuzi's **Nxwala Wilderness Area** (right).

*T*he **Ndumo Game Reserve** *(previous page) lies on the flood plain of the Pongola River and embraces several large pans where a great number of water-loving birds are to be found, some at the extreme southern limit of their ranges.*

KwaZulu-Natal's bushveld reserves are small compared with the great game parks of Africa further north, but just as rewarding. Wildlife abounds and the visitor is assured of seeing the **vervet monkey***, Cercopithecus aethiops (opposite, above right),*

and many species of antelope, including the gracile **nyala***, Tragelaphus angasii (opposite, above left).*

By the beginning of the century Africa's once widespread **white rhino***, Ceratotherium simum (above), had been reduced to a small group in the Umfolozi Game Reserve. But through the conservation efforts of the KwaZulu-Natal Nature Conservation Service, the animal is now thriving in reserves countrywide.*

The **Umfolozi Wilderness Trail** *(top and right) provides an unforgettable African experience.*

*The ever popular **Sodwana Bay** (right): a magical place of towering, forest-clad dunes that reach almost to the water's edge. Over weekends and during the holiday seasons, the bay becomes a hive of activity, its tranquillity shattered by the numerous anglers, divers and ski-boat enthusiasts descending on its shores. KwaZulu-Natal's northern coast, which offers some of the finest offshore angling spots, is a mecca for South Africa's considerable game-fishing fraternity:*

*more and more visitors are finding their relaxation in an underwater world. Here, time has a different quality as the diver glides through the reefs and corals discovering the marine world of the **clown fish** (top left), and the brightly coloured **common starfish** (top right).*

*The northern Zululand coast is home to the **Tsonga people** who, using traditional methods, fish the estuaries and lagoons and glean shellfish from the intertidal zone (above).*

The shores and waters of the **St Lucia Estuary** on the north coast of KwaZulu-Natal form one of the world's great wetland wilderness environments, the iSimangaliso Wetland Park. Here, **lesser flamingoes**, Phoenicopterus minor, *(above)* flock in their thousands. Just one of the more than 350 bird species recorded in the iSimangaliso Park, they also share the rich habitat with a diverse mammal population that includes the **hippopotamus**, Hippopotamus amphibius, *(right top)*. Although this huge vegetarian spends most of its day wallowing in the water it comes ashore after sundown to graze, and it is a common – and rather disquieting – early morning experience to find the lawns around the St Lucia camps pitted with the mean-tempered and often dangerous, amphibious creature's deep, four-toed footprints.

Low, slanting light casts a shadow over Lake St Lucia's aptly named **Bird Island** *(right centre)*; as the sun sets, **anglers** stand silhouetted against the warm glow off the water *(right)*.

*T*he soft light of the rising sun lends grace to
Durban's **highrise buildings** (left). In the fore-
ground are the beachfront hotels of the Marine
Parade, which faces onto the warm, inviting waters
of the Indian Ocean. Early morning is also the time
for **fishermen** (above), while away from the waterfront the ubiquitous **minibus taxis** (top) begin
their daily haul of passengers. Durban is one of
the world's fastest growing cities, and its seaport
the country's largest.

*The tower-blocks of Durban's central business district form an anonymous backdrop to the crisp white hulls of the yachts and cruisers riding gently at anchor in the sheltered waters of the **Point Yacht Club** (above).*

Durban's origins lie in British colonialism and, to a lesser extent, in an early and abortive Boer attempt to create a lasting republic, though the Zulu-speaking people were the first to make their home in the area. Much later came the inden-

tured labourers from India to add a significant and attractively exotic element to the cultural mix.

*The **Indian Market** (top left) is one of the trading hubs of the city; here just about everything is on offer, including curry powders with such ominous names as 'Extra Special Hell Fire' and 'Father-in-Law Special'.*

*These **Indian ladies** (top right) are elegantly draped in traditional saris for a wedding, but the **headgear** of this ricksha puller (right) has little to do with Zulu culture.*

Unlike KwaZulu-Natal's northern shoreline, with its great, uninterrupted stretches of marine and coastal reserves, the coast south of Durban is very different – an endless chain of quiet, beach-hugging towns and attractive resorts.

While some holidaymakers find the wildness of the north coast the more inviting getaway, many others prefer the charm and sociability of such pictur-esque places as **Leisure Bay** (above) and **Ramsgate** (right). Each has its own, distinctive attraction; here, the fishing is good, the many lagoons and shark-netted bays provide safe bathing, while rocky headlands create breaks to draw **surfers** (top right) from far and wide. During the prime holiday seasons of Christmas and Easter these otherwise sleepy spots throng with upcountry visi-tors taking full advantage of the many, relatively inexpensive hotels, holiday cottages and camping and caravan parks. The casino lying just over the Eastern Cape border is also a powerful drawcard.

*S*tretching southwards from the endless holiday villages and resort complexes of KwaZulu-Natal's South Coast to the city of East London is a sparsely populated, rugged shoreline aptly known as the Wild Coast. Here, countless vessels from the time of the early explorers to the present have foundered, some of them disappearing without trace.

The Wild Coast is part of the traditional home of Xhosa-speaking people of South Africa – their fore-fathers having settled here somewhere near the

beginning of the 15th century. It is a largely impov-
erished land and like this **young girl** (left), most of
its people eke out a living as best they can. The
compelling beauty of a coastline pounded by **huge
waves** (top left) and dotted with idyllic bays, inlets
and rocky features, such as that of **Hole-in-the-Wall**
(above), barely masks a land badly degraded through
overuse, stripped of its trees (for fuel) by people who
have no alternative but to deplete the natural
resources upon which they depend.

*A close-up view of the **Hole-in-the-Wall** (above; see also previous page), where the ceaseless pounding of the surf has worn a spectacular tunnel through a detached cliff at the entrance to the bay.*

*The Wild Coast is characterized by steeply rounded hills, their deep valleys forming convoluted courses for the many rivers that make their way towards the warm Indian Ocean, often ending in blind estuaries. This attractive spot, at **Port St Johns** (left) is, typically, fringed by a cluster of holiday homes.*

*This **old woman** (top) in traditional garb and peacefully drawing at her long, bead-decorated pipe is not from the Wild Coast or its adjacent hinterland; her beadwork and general attire place her home much farther south, to the west of the country's only river port, East London. Formerly known as the Ciskei, one of the so-called independent states that were created by earlier administrations during the years of apartheid rule, the region is also a stronghold of the Xhosa-speaking people.*

*T*he coastal section of the Tsitsikamma National Park covers a rugged stretch of shoreline fringing the eastern part of the famed Garden Route. This is a wild and spectacularly beautiful coast, notable for the **powerful seas** (above) that pound the narrow, rocky shores at the foot of towering cliffs, and for the rivers, their waters stained brown from the slow decomposition of forest vegetation, that thread their way to the Indian Ocean through deep tree-clad ravines. One of the many such watercourses is the **Storms River** (left), at the mouth of which is cluster of **log cabins** (top right) and a camping site. A feature of the Tsitsikamma National Park is its **underwater trail** (top left), on which snorklers can explore the submarine world of small fish, sea anemones, starfish and a myriad other creatures. Storms River mouth is also the starting point of the renowned Otter Trail, a 41-kilometre hike through forest and fynbos to the lovely Nature's Valley area at the western limit of the Park.

*P*lettenberg Bay was until fairly recently a quiet refuge of holiday homes, and of permanent residences belonging to retired people of means; but the area has been 'discovered' and, today, it is a boom town of the vacation industry, one of the most fashionable of resorts and the place to be seen soaking up the summer sun. Its huge popularity among wealthier Johannesburg holidaymakers has earned it the nickname of 'Sandton-by-the-Sea', a reference to one of the more affluent areas to the north of the financial metropolis. Beyond the veneer, though, Plettenberg Bay retains its magic, offering superb **sandy beaches**, which comfortably, even gracefully, accommodate the summer and sporting crowds (top), and the timeless **Robberg** (above), standing guard to the west of the town. This massive sandstone promontory, extending four kilometres into the ocean, is a nature reserve. The most eye-catching man-made feature of 'Plett' is the **Beacon Isle** time-share complex (left).

The narrows formed by Knysna's imposing **Heads** (above) are a formidable challenge to mariners entering and leaving the safe haven of the **lagoon** (left centre) and many craft have come to grief in the treacherous currents that scour the rocky shoreline. The South African coast is not known for protected inlets and bays, and the placid waters of the lagoon have elevated the town of Knysna to the front rank of holiday resorts, popular for fishing and for a whole range of watersports, including yachting and skiing. The lagoon is also one of the few places in South Africa where one can hire a cruiser or house-boat for a holiday afloat.

Knysna is a bustling town of some 40 000 in-habitants, a figure that swells dramatically in the holiday months. But tranquillity is never far from hand, whether in a quiet backwater where water-birds such as this **dabchick**, Tachybaptus ruficollis, (top left) go about their business or along a **leaf-strewn path** (left) in the adjacent indigenous forest.

*T*here are so many truly wild and remote places in South Africa that for a permanently settled area actually to be named Wilderness seems incongruous, especially when the place of that name has nothing of the rugged, pristine quality usually associated with Africa. It is, rather, a tranquil network of meandering rivers and still, freshwater lakes separated by a low rise of dunes from a long stretch of creamy beach. But Wilderness it is, and here, as along much of the Garden Route coast, the natural systems have had to accommodate roads, powerlines, houses, holiday cottages and hotels such as the quaintly named **Faerie Knowe** (top left). Although there is much to justify the deep concern of conservationists there are places, however, where a visual harmony does exist between nature and man-made structures, for no-one could deny the charm of the gently curving rail bridge over the mouth of the **Kaaimans River** (above), or the tiny cluster of **cottages** on its banks a little upstream (left).

*T*he site of the modern town of Mossel Bay, has for long had a place in the affairs of man. Centuries ago, well before the first Portuguese sea-farers dropped anchor to take on fresh water and whatever provender they could find, the shores were the domain of indigenous Khoikhoi people, who combed the rocks to gather the mussels that were eventually to lend their name to a thriving little fishing village. In recent years, however, Mossel Bay has grown rapidly to become a sizeable town, embracing industries that made their appearance after the discovery of offshore oil reserves. The town's protected **harbour** (top left) and this old **church** (top right) appear to belie these developments, while the **craggy bluff** (left) to the west of the town, deeply pitted at its base with wave-hewn caves, seems impervious to all but the steady forces of nature.

The view inland from Mossel Bay, where the not-too-distant **Outeniqua Mountains** (above) bar easy access to the hinterland in the Little Karoo.

*T*he Outeniqua Mountains run parallel to the coast for virtually the entire length of the Garden Route, their high ridges and peaks effectively blocking the inland progress of moisture-laden clouds moving in off the sea. For this reason the Garden Route is one of the better watered regions of South Africa, while the comparatively rain-starved Little Karoo to the north of the range begins to show the dry harshness that characterizes so much of the country's interior. This is farming country, a land of

sheep and horses, of fruit and grapes grown under irrigation, of small towns and mission stations such as that at **Zoar** (right), of fiery-tipped **aloes** (above) and the **ostrich**, Struthio camelus, (right centre) easily domesticated and for a time, at the end of the last century, the focus of a lucrative industry based on the fashion world's demand for the bird's feathers. But perhaps the best known of the Little Karoo's attractions are the **Cango Caves** (top right), a limestone fantasia of stalagmites and stalactites.

The Great Karoo is a vast semi-arid basin extending northwards from the Swartberg range to the southern Free State, and from Namaqualand in the west across the interior to the northern parts of the Eastern Cape. Sheep, goats and cattle find sustenance in the small-leaved scrubby vegetation of the mostly flat, featureless plains. It is the sort of country where roads run as straight as a die and seem to disappear in a shimmering heat haze at the point of infinity, but in parts the visual monotony is relieved by tumbles of dolomitic 'koppies' and ridges, such as those fringing the **Valley of Desolation** (left) near **Graaff-Reinet** (above). The town has a history dating back to the mid-18th century and, happily, many of its old fine buildings have survived – although some have found a very different use from that originally intended. For example, the old Drostdy (or magistrate's residence) and an adjacent row of painstakingly **restored cottages** (top) now serve as a charming country hotel.

*T*he Augrabies Falls National Park straddles the Gariep (Orange) in the far Northern Cape. Although this might seem a barren land, a closer look reveals an intriguing web of plants and animals that have adapted to the **arid terrain** (above). These **suricates,** Suricata suricatta (top), are social creatures, often sharing communal burrows. The **quiver tree,** Aloe dichotoma (left), has a smooth bark and small leaves clustered at the tips of bare branches, characteristics that limit the loss of moisture.

*T*he name Augrabies comes from a local phrase meaning 'great water', for it is here that the mighty Gariep (Orange) River is reluctantly channelled through a series of rapids before leaping the final 56-metre-drop into the narrow gorge below. In all, the river falls some 200 metres here. The **Augrabies** (top and right) is an awesome sight throughout the year but especially in times of heavy rains upstream. A familiar sight in this rocky terrain is the **klipspringer**, Oreotragus oreotragus (above).

*T*he black-and-white facial marking and long, straight horns allow easy identification of the **gemsbok**, Oryx gazella *(above)*. This large antelope is found in the dry western parts of South Africa, and in Botswana and in Namibia, where it is well adapted to its arid habitat: it is able to survive almost indefinitely without access to surface water, and to withstand temperatures which can soar to 40 °C or more. The antelope is frequently seen in the vast Kgalagadi Transfrontier Park, a wedge

of desert-type terrain, in the extreme north west of South Africa. The park offers an unforgettable experience of dry Africa, and superb game-viewing from the untarred road that runs along the banks of the mostly waterless Auob River between the two comfortable camps of Mata Mata and Twee Rivieren. The Kgalagadi Transfrontier Park is well known for its **lions**, Pantherea leo *(above)*, which have distinctively dark, heavy manes and for its birds of prey, including these nocturnal **whitefaced owls**, Otus leucotis *(top)*.

*W*ater is a precious commodity in Africa, but especially so in the semi-desert grassland savanna of the Kgalagadi Transfrontier Park, which is devoid of permanent natural supplies. Excellent game-viewing opportunities, however, are provided by artificial waterholes and here a juvenile **pale chanting goshawk**, Melierax canorus, enjoys a bath (top left), while a herd of springbok, Antidorcas marsupialis (right), come down to slake their thirst, a few keeping a lookout for danger.

Lions are mostly nocturnal and will spend the day snoozing (top), but towards evening and after much stretching and yawning they will rise and begin to take a keen interest in hunting. In the Kalahari, springbok are their main prey, but they also favour **gemsbok** (left), although they treat this antelope with great respect: it has the weaponry to deliver a potentially mortal thrust with its rapier-like horns.

A **crowned plover**, Vanellus coronatus, (far left, below) ubiquitous resident of the wide, open veld.

*T*he main rest camp at **Twee Rivieren** (above)
seen over the rim of one of the Kalahari's
famous dunes, which derive their burnt hues from
iron oxide in the soil.

Two **secretarybirds**, Sagittarius serpentarius –
the common name stems from the large, quill-like
feathers that protrude from the back of the neck –
size each other up prior to a territorial skirmish
(left centre). Secretarybirds generally occur in pairs
and will defend large territories, some as much as

50 square kilometres in extent. They are often seen striding across open grasslands searching for prey. In another territorial display two **springbok rams** (left below) lock horns in a test of strength during the rutting season.

The large ears of the **bat-eared fox**, Otocyon megalotis, (left, top) bear witness to the animal's acute sense of hearing. While out foraging a bat-eared fox will often stop to 'focus' its ears on the ground as it listens for prey – insects, reptiles and rodents –

beneath the surface. When a possible food source is located it vigorously digs for it with its forepaws.

Large mammals have mostly disappeared from the **Richtersveld** (following page), a huge, often hilly, rock-strewn corner of the Northern Cape's Namaqualand region, but many smaller creatures – rodents, elephant shrews, reptiles and birds – have carved niches for themselves. This recently proclaimed national park is of particular interest to botanists because of its unique succulent plant life.

It is difficult to comprehend the power that once buckled and bent the earth's surface to form the Cedarberg, a range of mountains that thrusts skywards from the Namaqualand plain. At its highest point it rises more than 2 000 metres above sea level, and in its upper parts the rocks and crags have weathered over millions of years to create a weird, almost **surreal landscape** (above) of overhangs, towers and clefts, many of them with evocative names like **Maltese Cross** (top left), **Wolfberg Arch** (left) and **Wolfberg Cracks** (top right). The Cedarberg – the name comes from the Clanwilliam cedar tree, Widdringtonia cedarbergensis, *once common but now rare and protected (because of past exploitation)* – is a mecca for hikers, mountaineers and naturalists alike. This strange mountain wilderness is rich in plant life (a number of species occur only here) and in birds and mammals, including the secretive leopard, for which the region is a pilot sanctuary aimed at reducing conflict between man and cat.

A simple **herder's cottage** *(right) set against the low rise of the Cedarberg foothills. Life is harsh in this sparsely settled part of Namaqualand: rain falls reluctantly; temperatures can soar to 40 ℃ and more in summer to drop below zero in winter, when snow blankets the high peaks.*

*But in spring, when the bleak countryside briefly gives way to transient carpets of flowers, there are rich pickings for an **angulate tortoise**,* Chersina angulata, *(above) which browses on daisies.*

*N*amaqualand is a vast, arid, semi-desert coastal region that runs almost due north from the well-watered winelands of the Western Cape. This is a harsh, unforgiving land, but when the winter rains are good it relents, releasing one of the most spectacular floral displays to be seen anywhere in the world. The wild flowers last just a few brief weeks in spring and people come from far to witness the **vivid carpets of colour** (above and opposite) and the **delicate beauty** (top) of an individual bloom.

*Although the holiday industry is big business for property developers, commercial fishing is still at the heart of the West Coast economy. All along this stark and often windswept shore are picturesque little harbours from which, for generations, men have put to sea in small boats to harvest the cold waters. Some, such as these rock lobster smacks working out of **Elands Bay** (above), stay relatively close inshore, while other, more substantial craft – these trawlers in the harbour of **Laaiplek** (top right),*

*for instance – work the deeper offshore fishing grounds. **Trek fishing** (right) is a traditional, but environmentally contentious practice in which nets are rowed out from the shore and then back to form a wide semi-circle; the net is then drawn in by hand, effectively trapping fish in its decreasing arc.*

*The **Cape fur seal**, Arctocephalus pusillus, (top left) is a prolific breeder: it is estimated that there are more than a million of these highly social mammals in southern Africa's coastal waters.*

*F*ishing boats nudge each other gently as they lie at anchor in the harbour of **Lambert's Bay** (right), they and their crews enjoying a welcome respite from the violent wind-storms that lash the West Coast. The harbours provide only partial protection from the raging seas and the shore is littered with the remains of ships and small boats that have foundered. As always along such coasts, fact and fancy mingle to produce local legends of dark deeds and lost treasure. One such mystery surrounds the wreck of HMS Sybille, which went aground in heavy seas just south of Lambert's Bay. She was the port's guardship during the Anglo-Boer War and was allegedly carrying a fortune.

Children pose shyly (top left) in the tiny fishing community of **Paternoster**. For many of the region's people, **bokkems** (top right) – heavily salted and dried fish – is the main source of protein.

The huge colony of **Cape gannets**, Morus capensis, (above) located at Bird Island off Lambert's Bay.

*T*able Mountain towers in the background at Cape Town's much acclaimed and ever-popular **V&A Waterfront** (previous page). This exciting project has brought life back to the mother city's dockland: tasteful renovation of derelict sheds and warehouses has created a sparkling world of restaurants, theatres, hotels, pubs and speciality shops that draw people in their thousands.

The quays are alive with the sound of **busking musicians** (top right), playing everything from soulful blues to the classics, and live concerts at the Amphitheatre (opposite), where groups such as these minstrels perform. Fun can be found everywhere along the waterfront, and food is never far from hand, whether it be a tasty snack on an open terrace or haute cuisine in one of the top **restaurants** (top left). Liquid sustenance, too, is a vital ingredient in the recreational mix; one of the most popular watering holes in Cape Town, indeed in the entire country, is **Quay Four** (above).

When **Jan van Riebeeck** – his statue (top) presides over Adderley Street – landed at the foot of Table Mountain in April 1652 he could not have envisaged the beautiful city that was to grow around the bay. Among Cape Town's charms are the many fine period buildings that have survived the ravages of property developers; cobbled **Greenmarket Square** (right) – where busy flea-market stalls now jostle for shade beneath the leafy trees – and the ever present **flower sellers** (above).

*It is difficult to imagine that, at the turn of the century, the only buildings along the **Clifton** coast (left) were a hotel and a cluster of cottages at the foot of the cliffs. Today it is the country's Côte d'Azur, mantled entirely by cantilevered multi-million rand houses and apartments. The crescent beaches of Clifton, well protected from the nagging south-east wind, are hugely popular among sun-worshippers; so, too, are the shimmering sands of nearby **Camps Bay** (above and top) on a fine day.*

*T*he road around **Chapman's Peak** (right), carved
from the almost sheer cliffs, must rate as one of the
world's most scenic drives. The 600-metre-high cliffs
form the southern flank of **Hout Bay**, a fiercely independent town with strong ties to its fishing harbour
(above). The **copper leopard** overlooking the azure
waters of the bay (top right) frequently suffers the
abuse of seagulls, while **cyclists** (top left) suffer a stiff
hill-climb out of Hout Bay that is enough to take the
puff out of even the fittest pedal-power enthusiast.

*T*he view over **Cape Point** *(above), dramatic meeting place of False Bay's warm waters with the chillier ones of the Atlantic's Benguela Current. Earlier mariners knew the massive headland as the 'Cape of Storms'; English circumnavigator Sir Francis Drake took a kindlier view, referring to it as 'the fairest cape in the whole circumference of the earth'. The rocky headland of **The Cape of Good Hope** (left), where a pair of **African black oystercatchers**,* Haematopus moquini, *(top) have come to rest.*

F **ish Hoek** (above), a sleepy seaside town on
the western shores of False Bay, has a long,
sandy and very safe beach from which it derives
its great summer popularity. The steep roads that
feed the hillside homes are a good vantage point
from which to scan the bay for the whales that
come to the sheltered parts of the Western Cape
coastal region to mate and to give birth.

Only kilometres from Fish Hoek lies the village of
St James (top right), where the brightly coloured

bathing booths are reminders of earlier decades,
when decorum demanded utmost discretion. St James
is one of the very few False Bay beaches that
escapes the stinging summer southeaster.

Around the rocky promontory from St James is
Muizenberg (above), also noted for its safe bathing.
This once highly fashionable resort town fell from
favour, but the new pavilion, with its restaurants,
concert hall and surrounding pools, has done much
to restore the area's popularity.

As you move around the eastern face of Table Mountain you enter a world of comfortable suburbia, of vineyards and oak trees, and acres of Academe. Here lies **Groot Constantia** (top left), South Africa's oldest country estate, originally built (in the early 1700s) by the then governor of the Cape, Simon van der Stel, and today a state-owned winery and major tourist attraction. A little farther along the mountain are the botanic gardens at **Kirstenbosch** (above and top right), repository of South Africa's incomparable floral wealth. Almost adjacent to the gardens is the **University of Cape Town** (right and opposite, top), which must enjoy one of the most beautiful settings of any seat of learning anywhere in the world. The land on which it stands was part the original estate of Cecil John Rhodes – arch-Imperialist, mining magnate and, towards the end of the 19th century, premier of the Cape Colony. Rhodes's 'immense and brooding spirit' is captured in his **memorial** (opposite, top right), which faces north.

*The fine front gable (above) of **Schoongezicht** manor house on the historic Rustenberg wine estate, where wines have been made continuously since 1892 – so far as is known the longest uninterrupted working life of any of the wineland farms.*

*The scenery of the winelands is often spectacular, but few views can compare with that from the **Alto Estate** (right), which is renowned for its Alto Rouge, a full-bodied blend long regarded by many as one of the aristocrats among the Cape red wines.*

Stellenbosch is a beautiful town of oak-lined streets and gracious, well-proportioned buildings, many with the high white gables so characteristic of the Cape Dutch style, others displaying the elaborate wrought-iron ornamentation typical of Victorian times. It is also a university town where student-powered bicycles ease their way along the leafy avenues, seemingly in no hurry to deliver their charges. Before all else, though, Stellenbosch is the wine capital of the country.

The town is rich in places of interest, and a quiet stroll down **Dorp Street** (above) – where **Oom Samie se Winkel** (right), with its enchanting clutter of bric-a-brac is a landmark – is a delight indeed. Exploring, especially in the scorching heat of summer, can take its toll, but there is respite in many inviting **pubs and restaurants** (opposite, top right).

A suitably disguised local (opposite, top left) plays the part of Stellenbosch's founding father, **Simon van der Stel**, during a town festival.

*In the Western Cape, whether within the town limits of Stellenbosch and Paarl or out and about in the surrounding countryside, one is never far from the wine industry – and locals are justifiably proud of their vintages, which regularly win prizes at international shows. By its very nature wine farming is steeped in tradition, and any route through the vine-clothed countryside will reveal venerable old **homesteads** and their attendant outbuildings (right), where wine has been made*

for generations. Despite the deference to tradition, however, mechanization and modern technology are very much the tools of the farmer of today, although **horse-drawn implements** (top left) are sometimes still in evidence in older vineyards.

Another tradition of the Western Cape is a bredie or mutton casserole made from **waterblommetjies,** Aponogeton distachyos, prized water-plants which are harvested from shallow dams and vleis in the early spring (left).

*N*o visit to the Cape would be complete without a day spent exploring a wine route, either on one of the many bus tours on offer or by meandering through the country roads by car. The route through the **Franschhoek Valley** *(left),* named after the French Huguenot refugees who settled the region in the late 17th century, is probably the most picturesque, sheltered as it is by the high flanking granite walls of the Simonsberg and the Groot Drakenstein mountains.

For visitors, a leisurely restaurant lunch or a picnic under the pines at **Boschendal** *(top left),* is obligatory, as are a quick look at the **Huguenot Memorial** *(above),* a browse around the **antique shops** *(top right)* and, of course, visits to local cellars to taste their wares. And so the day passes pleasantly and without stress – except perhaps for the post-prandial drive back to town with a carload of precious liquid, a lighter wallet and the setting sun sending daggers of light into sensitive eyes.

*T*ulbagh dates back to the beginning of the 18th century, when the first Dutch settlers began to farm the region. Its growth was slow, and without much ado it moved quietly with the decades until one fateful night in September 1969, when the worst earthquake in South Africa's recorded history struck the Western Cape. Tulbagh was close to the centre of the tremor and many of its lovely old buildings came tumbling down. Fortunately only a few lives were lost, but much of the town lay in ruins.

With great determination Tulbagh's burgers, with the help of experts, set about rebuilding the place, lovingly restoring it to its former character. Today it is difficult to envisage that **Church Street** (above) and many other parts of the town had once been reduced to rubble.

Tulbagh, too, has its wine route and cool cellars such as those at **De Oude Drostdy** (top left) and the **Paddagang restaurant** (left) make the relatively long drive from Cape Town well worthwhile.

*T*he pretty town of **Hermanus** *(above) perches atop the cliffs of Walker Bay. Hermanus is easily accessible from Cape Town, which is only an hour's drive to the west and, as in so many coastal centres of the Western Cape, the olde-worlde charm of the place, with its elegant fringe of gracious homes and hotels coexists uneasily with the rash of newer developments. But Hermanus and its permanent residents cope comfortably, and amiably, with the summer vacationers who throng to such beaches as*

Voëlklip (top): for the business community, the
holiday season is much anticipated as it means
full hotels and restaurants and a few short weeks
of buoyant retail trade.

The **old harbour** (above) tucked into a cove
at the foot of the cliffs – a setting that would not
be out of place along the English coast – has long
since given up its working status to a modern harbour sited to the west of the town, and is now
a museum and national monument.

On a still day the charming little fishing hamlet of Arniston, with its picturesque **thatch-roofed cottages** (centre right) and **brilliant white dunes** (above), is idyllic, but when the winds howl, as they often do, the turquoise sea is whipped to a froth of whitecaps, the driving sands blast all in their path, and only the hardiest of locals venture abroad. The town has two names: one taken from the wreck of the Arniston, the other **Waenhuiskrans** (wagon house cliff), from the huge nearby cavern (right).

In recent years the towns and bays of the Western Cape coast have been drawing the crowds during the colder months as well, for this is 'whale watch' time, when the **southern right whale**, Balaena glacialis, (top right) shelters in the shallow, protected waters to mate and to give birth. The sight – and sound – of these leviathans breaching and slapping the water with their tails is unforgettable.

The lighthouse at **Cape Agulhas** (overleaf), the southernmost point of the African continent.

INDEX

PHOTOGRAPHIC CREDITS

Shaen Adey: frontispiece, pages 8 above right, 72, 76, 101 above right]; **Andrew Bannister:** pages 108 above; **Anthony Bannister:** pages 30 above right, 33 above, 51, 78 below, 116/117 [GI], 125 above left [GI]; **Daryl Balfour:** pages 10 below, 120 left, 144, 145, 146, 147 below and top right, 149, 151 above left, 157 top; **Guy Cunningham:** pages 28 below [GI], 29 [GI]; **Daphne Carew:** page 114 middle [GI]; **Roger de la Harpe/AFRICA IMAGERY.COM:** pages 27 above right, 38 top, 47 above left, 57 below, 62 [AB/GI], 65, 68, 69, 77 above right, 78 above left [GI],79, 81 below, 84 above right [GI], 85, 87 above, 93 below, 98 above right [GI], 99 [GI], 101 above left, 106, 108 below, 113 above; **Gerald Cubitt:** cover; **Nigel Dennis/AFRICA IMAGERY.COM:** pages 53 above left, 58 above [GI], 73 middle, 80, 81 above [GI], 96 top, 112 right, 114 below [AB/GI]; **Wendy Dennis/AFRICA IMAGERY.COM:** title page; **Gerhardus du Plessis:** page 88 above [Photo Access]; **Richard du Toit:** pages 38 middle [GI], 38 bottom [GI], 39 [GI], 42 below [GI], 47 below; **Aubrey Elliott:** pages 66 below, 67; **Paul Funston:** pages 40/41 [GI], 42 above left [GI]; **Malcolm Funston:** page 71 [GI]; **Ken Gerhardt:** pages 154 [Photo Access], 155 below [Photo Access], 156 [Photo Access]; **Clem Haagner:** page 8 left [GI]; **Lesley Hay:** pages 27 above left [GI]; **Doreen Hemp:** pages 11, 12, 23 above; **Lex Hes:** pages 36, 37, 42 above right, 43, 44, 45, 46, 47 above right; **Werner Kaufmann:** pages 157 middle [Photo Access]; **Walter Knirr:** pages 15, 19 above left and below, 20 below, 22, 23 below, 27 below, 30 below, 31, 32, 50 below, 52, 54/55, 61 right, 63, 83 below, 86, 87 below, 98 above, 102, 103 below, 104, 105 above, 123, 126 below, 127, 134, 137, 138, 140, 141 below, 143 below, 157 below; **Peter Lawson:** page 30 above left [Photo Access]; **John McKinnell:** pages 59, 60/61, 103 top; **KwaZulu-Natal Nature Conservation Service:** pages 53 below and above right, 56, 58 below, 70, 73 below and above, 77 below, 78 above right, [all Roger de la Harpe], page 57 above [Shaen Adey]; **Robert C. Nunning-**ton: pages 74/75 [GI], 77 above left [GI], 109, 113 below [GI]; **John Paisley:** page 91 above [Photo Access]; **Colin Paterson-Jones:** pages 100, 101 below, 107 below, 112 left, 114 top, 139 above, 142; **Peter Pickford:** spine, pages 28 above, 35, 91 below, 124, 125 above right and below, 126 above; **Herman Potgieter:** pages 17, 18 [GI], 24, 25, 66 above, 81 middle, 82, 83 above, 89 [GI], 94 [GI], 95 below [GI]; **Eric Reisinger:** page 41 [GI]; **Phillip Richardson:** page 110 [GI]; **Joan Ryder:** page 50 above [GI]; **Lorna Stanton:** pages 16 above left [GI], 33 below [GI]; **David Steele:** pages 96 middle [Photo Access], 111 top, [Photo Access], 113 [Photo Access], 115 [Photo Access], 152 below [Photo Access], 153 [Photo Access], 155 above [Photo Access]; **Austin Stevens:** page 107 above [Photo Access]; **Images of Africa:** title page, pages 9, 95 above, 128/129, 130, 131, 131 above left [GI], 132 above, 135, 136 above right, 139 below, 141 above, 143 above left, 147 above left and middle, 148 below, 150, 151 above right and below; **August Sycholt:** pages 10 above, 16 below, 64, 103 middle, 158; **Erhardt Thiel:** pages 9, 128/129, 132 above, 136 above right, 141 above, 143 above left, 147 above left and middle, 148 below, 150, 151 above right and below; **Lisa Trocchi:** pages 14 above [GI], 16 above right [GI]; **Lorraine van Hooff:** pages 84 above right [Photo Access], 84 below [Photo Access]; **Mark van Aardt:** imprint page, pages 19 above right, 20 above, 21, 26, 96 below, 97, 98 below, 105 below, 139 below, 143 above right; **Hein von Hörsten:** pages 92 [GI], 120/121 [GI], 122 below [GI], 132 below, 133, 135, 136 above left [GI], 148 above [GI], 149 [GI]; **Patrick Wagner:** pages 118 [Photo Access], 119 [Photo Access]; **Keith Young:** pages 88 below [Photo Access], 93 above left, 122 above, 136 below, 152 above.

Copyright in the above photographs rests with the photographers and/or their appointed agents.

[GI = Gallo Images]